Just Like Lee

By LaShanta Smith

Copyright © 2025, Lashanta Smith

All rights reserved. No part of this publication may be reproduced, stored in a retrieval system or transmitted in any form or by any means, electronic, mechanical, photocopying, recording or otherwise, without prior written permission from the publisher, Engraving Your Views. All rights, reserved, including the right to reproduce this book or portions thereof in any form

ISBN HARDCOVER: 9798998638947

Dedication

To my mother, my children, and my grandchildren, I dedicate Lessons Learned to you.

To my mother - your love, guidance, and strength shaped me into the woman I am today.

Your sacrifices and wisdom taught me how to rise above challenges and to keep faith at the center of my life.

To my children - you are my motivation and my joy. You remind me daily of the

importance of perseverance, love, and hope.

To my grandchildren - you are my inspiration for the future, a living reminder that everything I've endured was worth it. You are my greatest blessing and my legacy.

This book is for you. I will always love you.

- LaShanta Smith

Author Bio

My name is LaShanta Smith, and I am an early childhood educator, author, and advocate for inclusive learning. For nearly three decades, I have dedicated my life to working with children of all abilities and creating spaces where every child feels valued, supported, and inspired to shine.

My passion comes not only from my professional experience, but also from my journey as a mother, grandmother, and caregiver to children with unique needs. These roles have shaped who I am and strengthened my belief that every child deserves a safe place to learn, grow, and be celebrated for who they are.

Through my writing, I share stories that highlight kindness, empathy, and belonging. My goal is to encourage families, educators, and communities to start meaningful conversations with children-conversations that build confidence, acceptance, and compassion.

More than anything, I want my work to leave a lasting impact on children and families. This is not just my career—it is my calling, my purpose, and the legacy I hope to leave behind.

Table of Contents

Dedication 3

Chapter 1: Meet Lee 6

Chapter 2: High School Years 8

Chapter 3: Transition Program (18–22) 9

Chapter 4: Everyday Life with Lee 11

Chapter 5: Looking Around, Looking Ahead 13

Chapter 6: After the Program 15

Chapter 7: You Belong Too 17

Parent & Educator Resources 18

Chapter 1: Meet Lee

This is Lee.

Lee is eighteen years old. He is quiet, shy, and full of love. If you met him today, he would probably smile softly and call you his friend, because Lee believes that everyone he meets is his friend. His heart is bigger than his words.

Lee is the kind of person who notices things that others don't. He notices the way music feels in his chest when the beat drops. He notices the colors in a painting and how each brush stroke can change the whole picture. He notices cars, too—especially the shiny ones that rumble when the engine starts.

Lee dreams about DJing, painting, and one day owning an auto body shop. His dreams are big, even if he doesn't always say them out loud.

At home, Lee is surrounded by family who loves him. His cousins mean the world to him. He laughs with them, plays with them, and sometimes just sits quietly, watching what they do. But Lee also sees the differences between himself and his cousins. They are driving cars, going away to college, and talking about their future jobs.

Lee wonders, Why can't I do that too?

Sometimes those thoughts make him feel left out. It can be confusing when you don't understand why life feels different for you than it does for the people you love.

But here's what makes Lee special: even when he doesn't understand everything, he never gives up on trying. His smile, his hugs, and his gentle spirit remind everyone around him that he belongs—just as he is.

Lee is at a turning point in his life. High school has ended, and now he is stepping into something new: a program that will help him learn how to be more independent, how to work, and how to grow into adulthood in his own way.

This is Lee's story. It is about his dreams, his challenges, and his journey to becoming the young man he is meant to be. And along the way, it is a story for every parent, teacher, and student who needs to hear: You are not alone. You belong.

Chapter 2: High School Years

High school is supposed to be a time of discovery. For some kids, it's about sports, making friends, or preparing for college. For Lee, high school was different.

Lee liked school, but not always in the same way as his cousins or classmates. He enjoyed certain classes, especially when they gave him space to move, create, or listen to music. He smiled when teachers praised his effort, even if the work was harder for him.

But high school also came with challenges. The noise of crowded hallways could be overwhelming. The fast pace of lessons sometimes left him behind. He worked hard, but he often wondered why things that seemed easy for others were more difficult for him.

Still, Lee never gave up. He walked into class every morning, ready to try again. He greeted people with his shy smile, and he believed they were all his friends. His teachers noticed how kind he was, how he wanted to help, and how his laughter could brighten up the room.

Graduation was a big day for Lee. He wore his cap and gown with pride, and his family cheered as he crossed the stage. For Lee, it wasn't just about finishing high school—it was about proving to himself and everyone else that he could do it.

But after the celebration ended, Lee felt something he hadn't expected: uncertainty. His cousins were talking about driving, college, and moving into dorms. Lee looked at them and thought, What about me? Where do I go next?

This is where Lee's story took a new turn. Instead of heading to college, Lee enrolled in something different, something built just for young adults like him: a transition program.

Chapter 3: Transition Program (18–22)

After high school, Lee didn't go to college like some of his cousins. Instead, he started something called a transition program.

A transition program is for young adults with disabilities who are between 18 and 22 years old. It's a place where students can keep learning, but the lessons are different. Instead of math tests or science labs, the focus is on real-life skills.

Lee's first day in the program was a mix of nerves and excitement. He walked into the building wearing his red T-shirt, jeans, and sneakers, his usual style. The doors had a sign that read 'Transition Program 18–22.' Inside, there were other students his age. Some looked nervous, just like him. Others smiled and waved, and Lee, of course, waved back.

In the transition program, Lee began to learn things that would help him live more independently:
- Cooking simple meals like pasta or scrambled eggs.
- Shopping for groceries and paying at the checkout.
- Budgeting money so he could buy the things he wanted from Amazon without running out too fast.
- Travel training — practicing how to ride the bus or find his way around town.

Lee also had chances to try different jobs. He helped stock shelves in a store, cleaned tables in a cafeteria, and learned how to organize supplies in a classroom. Not every job was easy, but each one taught him something new about what he could do.

The best part of the program was being with other students who understood. Lee made friends who were also learning to cook, budget, and prepare for jobs. They encouraged one another, laughed together, and celebrated small victories.

Lee still thought about his cousins—about cars, college, and independence—but he was beginning to see that his path was just as important, even if it looked different. This was the start of Lee's journey into adulthood.

Chapter 4: Everyday Life with Lee

Life in the transition program gave Lee structure, but what made his days special were the little things that showed who he really was.

Every morning, Lee got ready for school with his same gentle routine. He liked putting on his red T-shirt and sneakers—it made him feel comfortable and confident. He carried his phone, ready to listen to music whenever he had a chance.

Music was always with him. If you gave Lee a pair of headphones, his whole face lit up. He loved the rhythm of the beat, the way it filled the air and made him want to move. Music helped him relax when he felt nervous, and it gave him energy when he needed a boost.

Lee also loved to paint. His artwork was bright, colorful, and bold, just like his imagination. With a brush in his hand, he could show feelings that were sometimes hard to put into words.

And then there were cars. Lee could spot his favorite models from far away. He knew the sound of an engine before most people even noticed the car. His dream of owning an auto body shop never left his mind.

Of course, Lee had his everyday favorites too. One of the highlights of his week was when an Amazon package arrived. It could be something small, like headphones or a new shirt, but to Lee, it felt like a big reward. He smiled with pride every time he opened a box that had his name on it.

What made Lee truly special, though, wasn't just what he liked—it was who he was. Lee believed in people. He thought everyone he met was a friend. If someone smiled at him, he smiled back. If someone needed help, he was the first to step forward.

Sometimes, Lee struggled with big emotions. When he got frustrated or confused, he needed extra support from teachers or family to calm down. But even on tough days, his kindness always came through.

Lee's everyday life was simple, but it was filled with love, laughter, and dreams. And every day, he was learning more about how to be independent and how to shine as himself.

Chapter 5: Looking Around, Looking Ahead

Sometimes, Lee couldn't help but notice the differences between himself and the people around him.

His cousins were busy learning to drive. Some of them were in college, moving into dorms, and talking about careers. Others were working jobs, saving money, and planning their futures.

Lee watched with quiet eyes. He wondered, Why can't I do that too?

It was hard for him to understand why his path looked different. Why he wasn't filling out college applications, or getting car keys, or planning to move away from home.

These moments sometimes left Lee feeling left out, even though no one meant to make him feel that way. It wasn't jealousy—it was confusion. He loved his cousins deeply and wanted to cheer them on. But at the same time, he wanted to belong in the same way they did.

The truth is, many young adults with disabilities feel this way. They see their peers moving forward in ways that seem "normal," while their own path looks unfamiliar. It can be painful, and it can make the future feel uncertain.

But Lee was learning an important lesson: his journey mattered, too.

In his transition program, Lee was gaining skills that would help him live as independently as possible.

He was practicing real-world jobs, managing money, and learning how to care for himself. These things might not look the same as going to college or moving into a dorm, but they were just as valuable.

Lee's family reminded him often: "Your path is yours, and it is enough."

Little by little, Lee began to understand. Belonging didn't mean doing the exact same things as his cousins. Belonging meant being accepted, supported, and celebrated for who he was.

And when Lee looked ahead, he saw possibilities: working a job he enjoyed, saving money for the things he loved, maybe even DJing at a party or painting a masterpiece that made people smile.

His future might look different—but different could still be amazing.

Chapter 6: After the Program

The transition program doesn't last forever. It is designed for students ages 18 to 22. After that, young adults move on to the next step in their lives.

For Lee, thinking about "what's next" felt both exciting and scary. He had learned so much in the program: how to cook, how to budget money, how to ride the bus, and how to practice different jobs.

But he wondered—what would happen when the program was over?

This question is one that many families face. When the school bus stops coming, and the safety of the classroom is gone, it can feel like stepping into the unknown.

Lee's teachers and family helped him prepare by talking about options. Some students move into supported living programs, where they share an apartment with others and have staff to help them stay safe and independent. Others find jobs that fit their strengths, like stocking shelves, preparing food, or helping in offices. Some volunteer, building skills and confidence while giving back to their community.

Lee dreamed of working with music, painting, or cars. His family encouraged him to keep those dreams alive while also exploring jobs that matched his abilities. They reminded him that success doesn't look the same for everyone.

The most important part was this: Lee would not be alone. Even after the program ended, he would still have people cheering him on—his family, his teachers, and his community.

Life after the transition program isn't always easy. There are challenges, gaps in services, and moments of uncertainty. But there is also hope, possibility, and pride. Lee's journey showed that every young adult deserves a future where they feel safe, included, and valued.

As Lee thought about what came next, he didn't have all the answers. But he knew one thing for sure: he was ready to keep trying.

Chapter 7: You Belong Too

Lee's story is just one story. But it is also the story of many young adults who are finding their way in a world that doesn't always understand them.

If you are a young adult reading this, you might sometimes feel like Lee—watching others drive cars, go to college, or move away from home while you take a different path. It's okay to feel confused, or even sad, about those differences. But remember this: your path matters. You belong in this world exactly as you are.

If you are a parent reading this, you might worry about your child's future. You may feel overwhelmed with the challenges, or wonder if you're doing enough. Lee's story is here to remind you that you are not alone. Other families walk this road too, and there are programs, communities, and people who want to help.

Lee's life is proof that success doesn't have to look like everyone else's. Success can mean cooking your own meals, learning to budget, working a job you enjoy, or sharing your gifts—like music, painting, or kindness—with the world.

Most of all, Lee reminds us that belonging is not about fitting in. Belonging is about being loved, supported, and celebrated for who you are.

So whether you are a young adult, a parent, or a teacher, let Lee's story stay with you. Hold on to the truth that everyone has something valuable to give, and everyone deserves to feel included.

Just like Lee, you belong too.

Parent & Educator Resources

What is a Transition Program?

A transition program is designed for young adults with disabilities, usually between the ages of 18–22. It focuses on teaching real-life skills that help students prepare for adulthood, including:

- Cooking and meal planning
- Budgeting and money management
- Using public transportation
- Job training and workplace skills
- Social skills and independence

Tips for Parents
- Celebrate progress, not perfection. Every small step—learning to ride the bus, cooking a meal, or finishing a work shift—is a big success.

- Explore strengths. Notice what your child enjoys (music, art, cars, technology) and look for ways to build those interests into job or volunteer opportunities.

- Stay connected. Transition can feel isolating. Join parent support groups, connect with other families, and ask your school or community about resources.

- Plan early. Start talking about what comes after the program well before graduation, so the change feels less overwhelming.

Tips for Educators
- Focus on independence. Teach skills students can use outside the classroom, in real life.
- Encourage self-advocacy. Give students chances to speak up about what they want and need.
- Model inclusion. Create classroom environments where all abilities are respected and celebrated.

- Partner with families. Share progress, struggles, and ideas openly. Families and teachers are a team.

Helpful Resources
- The Arc of the United States: Support, advocacy, and resources for individuals with disabilities.
- Easterseals: Services for children and adults with disabilities, including job training.
- Transition Coalition: Tools and training for families and educators about transition planning.
- Local School District Programs: Ask about community-based transition programs near you.
- Parent Support Groups: Online and local groups provide connection and encouragement.

Final Encouragement
Transitioning into adulthood can feel overwhelming—for both young adults and their families. But remember, you are not alone. Support, community, and hope are out there.

Lee's story is a reminder: every young adult deserves to live a life where they are safe, included, and valued. And with love, patience, and the right supports, amazing things are possible.